THE
POWER OF CHOICE

Foreword by

MUMINA BONAYA

Chief Administrative Secretary,
Ministry of Education, Kenya

Other Books by John Abdub

The Journey To Self-Realization

THE

POWER OF CHOICE

A Choice Guide to Success

JOHN ABDUB WAKO

Print-on-Demand Edition on Amazon by Mystery Publishers – 2020
Kindle Edition by Mystery Books – 2020
This paperback Edition – 2020

Published by:
Mystery Publishers Ltd,
P.O. Box 18016 – 20100,
Nakuru, Kenya.
Tel: 254 718 429 184
Website: www.mysterypublisherslimited.com
Email: info@mysterypublisherslimited.com

To contact the author:
Tel: +254 710 420329
Email: johnabdub@gmail.com

Typeset in Garamond Pt.12 by Mystery Publishers

Available from Mystery Bookstore, Amazon, Kindle and other online retailers.

DEDICATION

This Great Book is dedicated to my family, especially my grandparents, thank you. To the young people and parents who are full of dreams and ambitions. To the whole world—unite to make the future generation succeed; we frequently need new impulses to drive us even higher.

Not forgetting all those who chose to respect life—in life there is the world of possibilities and greatness. Above all, live according to God's purpose in your life. Yes, you can fly higher like an eagle. Have a good time as you read this inspirational piece on choice and make the best choice out of it.

Choose to be the best of the best and not the least of the best!

CONTENTS

FOREWORD

WHEN I SAT down to write this foreword, I remembered a story I once read. In the story, a king received two magnificent falcons as a gift. He gave the precious birds to his head falconer to be trained. After months of training, the falconer shared with the king the progress of the falcons'. He reported that while one of the falcons was flying majestically, soaring high in the sky, the other bird had not moved from its branch since the day it arrived. This worried the king. Healers and sorcerers from all over the kingdom were summoned to tend to the falcon but no one could make the bird fly—the bird remained on its perch. In the end, a farmer was brought on board to help sort out the matter. The next morning, the king was thrilled to see the falcon soaring high above the palace gardens. This was a miracle and the king wanted to know how it happened. The king asked the farmer, "How did you make the falcon fly?" With his head bowed, the farmer said to the king, "It was very easy, Your Highness. I simply cut the branch where the bird was sitting."

The moral of the story is that we are all made to fly; to realise our incredible potentials as human beings, BUT what brings about the whole difference, as we observed with the two birds and our everyday life, is the choices we make. At times we sit on our 'branches', clinging to the things that are familiar to us as we are made to believe it is comfortable staying where we are, and not embracing other options that we may have.

John Abdub Wako, in *The Power of Choice,* posits that we all have the power in our hands and CHOICE to decide where we want to be and what we want to become. John made a choice of touching the lives of many through writing and art. Of course, before taking this path, he had an option of not doing anything about his talent and desire to reach out to the world through writing, but he chose to ACT. *The Power of Choice* mirrors how life is premised on choices that we make every day.

In the ten powerful choices addressed in the book, I got more intrigued by how the need of NOW was well expounded on. Nothing happens unless you choose to act now. You can either stay where you are and remain stuck and stagnant, wishing that things would go back to how they were or leap ahead by making a new choice that transforms your life.

As a pastoralist girl, I grew up in a patriarchal setup where cultural norms and practices were very strong. This meant that I had very limited choices over what to do with my life. Girls' education is not valued; nor is it a priority. As soon as a suitor shows up for your hand in marriage, your education ends there and marriage takes precedence; it does not matter your age or the dreams you hold in life—you are expected to comply. This was the situation that confronted my desire to get educated, so I made a choice, a choice that didn't sit well with my own mum and other relatives at that time. However, I needed to make that 'unpopular' choice THEN, for me to become who I am TODAY.

When we make a conscious choice about something in our lives, we release energy into the universe and our entire life experiences a shift for the better. All that is required is you choose that which makes you come to life. Make the choice.

I hope and believe that this book will be of great impact in our generation today and those to come as they watch over the choices they make in life. I pray and hope that the choice we make after reading this powerful book will be a positive choice full of hope and power in creating a greater destiny.

Thank you John for being thoughtful in making a difference in the lives of many through this book.

Ms. Mumina Bonaya
Chief Administrative Secretary,
Ministry of Education, Kenya

PREFACE

Our Existence Comprises a network of choices that we make every day. This could range from drinking tea in the morning to attending to making important life decisions. Whether you decide to attend to your best class or decide to take yourself for a trip and miss the class or decide to sleep, it all boils down to personal choice. You are the one to take control of your life. As you make the choices, be ready to bear the consequences. In spite of our parents making most of our decisions for our better and brighter future when we are young, we start learning how to choose between the options placed in front of us and make decisions. Our lives are a series of choices we make. We live with the choices for the rest of our lives. Our dreams are valid but they are determined by the type of choices we make daily. Show me the boat you are sailing on and I will tell you where you are heading to. Our choice gives us a reflection of our future.

The past can't be altered yet it offers you an insight into the mistakes you made. The present is a gift you need to make the best of and the core of your future comprises each and every single decision you have ever taken.

This is the book that will most inspire you to focus on your ability to make decisions. It is not just any decision but the best decision that will shape your academics, dream career, business, and life at large.

Choose to be a positive thinker; desire greatness and do great things,   be determined; know to say yes and no at the right time; always focus on your ultimate purpose in this world; be confident to face the world at every stage of life; network wisely; and above all, be consistent in all the extraordinary things you do.

All this defines a true warrior of success at any age. Nevertheless, success has no age or time limit. It's a process of gradual achievement. Therefore, you can achieve anything at any age as long as you choose wisely. There are many PhD holders in their 20's, eighteen-year-old company CEOs, innovative fifteen year-olds, seven-year-old authors as well as ten-year-old great scientists. Therefore, you should not limit your dream to 'when I grow up ...' We do put limits to our unlimited potentials at different times of our life. You can be who you want to be at any time as long you decide whether it is today or later.

ACKNOWLEDGEMENT

It's With Great honour that I thank the Almighty God for the wisdom, guidance and for all the wonderful mercies and blessings He has had over me. I am what I am today because of His grace.

I would also like to sincerely give gratitude to several people for their immense contributions in shaping my personality: my parents Joseph Wako Duba and Roseanna Aroba for their endless support in my studies and my siblings George Galgallo, Stephen Roba, Samuel Sora, and Maria Orge.

I am grateful to all my teachers from Manyatta Jillo Nursery and Primary School, Mokowe Primary School in Lamu, Dona Olinda Academy, Kenya Navy Primary School, and Moi Forces Academy, Mombasa, for their grand involvement in imparting knowledge in me and showing me the importance of education.

I thank Hatua Likoni Organization for sponsoring my university studies—you are a God-sent gift.

With gratitude, I thank all my friends and colleagues who inspired, touched, advised me, and for being there for me.

1

INTRODUCTION

Defining Success

SUCCESS IS THE unfolding blueprint of our life and moving on to a better tomorrow. It is a process and not a one-time event. It is neither a place nor a destiny, or a plan. It means being triumphant in whatever we want to do that makes sense to us. That is, taking responsibility for our lives since we have the power of choice with us.

However, each individual may define success differently depending on their backgrounds. There are those who term success as getting wealth, having a good relationship, winning a leadership position, fame, passing exams, etc. Is success about having money? Is it about having fun, or about finding spiritual enlightenment? Is it about finding love, or having great friends and family? Is it about finding contentment, or just living in the moment? Is it all of the above? These are questions that give us the viewpoint for what success means to us.

Being successful is determined by achieving your goals and dreams. It does not matter how small your achievement is. Remember success is a process and the small achievements lead to greater and bigger achievements. Always live to be thankful for the steps of success you have achieved.

In order to emerge victorious and make right choices, we need to have guiding principles which are the pillars to our success. The pillars ought to be made of concrete materials in order to help the pillars to last and stand the storms of life. The key raw materials for the pillars include personal choice, parenting, and attitude.

Personal Choice

As human beings, we are the most blessed among the entire creation. It's only human beings who have multiple choices to make, unlike other creatures. For instance, during the hot dry season, bees are unable to work or fly due to high temperatures which weaken them thus cluster themselves around the hives. If you suggest to the bees to work during hot temperatures, they will ignore that advice as they have no alternative choice. They are driven by instinct like all animals.

Human beings have the power of choice under all circumstances. We are not like robots, or stuck like a tree, using up all nourishment and, with nothing left, die because we cannot change locations. Human beings can change positions, directions, as well as destinations, depending on their choice in order to get whatever they want. As human beings, we have the power of choice. Why not use that power bestowed on us?

The power of choice is the single force that controls the quality of your life. It's the only power that you have that can change everything in your life. The past doesn't matter. You don't have to be sad, you can choose happiness. You don't have to be afraid, you can choose courage. You don't need to be discouraged, you can choose hope. You don't need to be hurried, you can choose calmness. You don't have to fail, you can choose success. You don't have to be lonely, you can choose love. You don't have to be defeated, you can choose victory.

Every aspect of your life is influenced by the choices you make, even doing nothing. Your happiness, health, relationships, career, attitude, education, lifestyle, and character, are just some of the many aspects impacted. At any moment we have hundreds of decision making options, some significant and some seemingly insignificant. Too often we operate automatically by doing things as a habit rather than by making conscious decisions. In this case, we find ourselves making lots of mistakes that we may come to regret later.

We can begin by reflecting on moments in our lives that we have made decisions that have impacted our future. Each decision, no matter how insignificant, impacts on who we are, what we are doing, and the relationships we choose.

Although you may want all of your decisions to be perfect, it's impossible to go through life without making some bad ones. This process is part of our learning curve. We will actually learn more from bad decisions than from the good ones.

Regardless of our past choices, we are always free to make new ones. This is how we make corrections. We have the right and the ability to control our thoughts; thus, for us to change our direction, we must change our thinking.

Fear of the wrong choice can inhibit us from making any choice. Yet, not making a decision is also a choice. The path of success and accomplishment requires making choices, not avoiding them.

There are no guarantees. Avoiding all bad choices is not possible. However, there are steps we can take to make the best possible choices. Remember, bad choices can be corrected or mitigated by following up with better ones.

It is very easy to see how people have been programmed to believe things that are not true or in their best interest. Things that they know, on some level, are not true. However, they decide not to think for themselves or act on their own inner knowledge. We are all connected to universal intelligence. Deep within each of us is the knowledge that we need to understand what we need to know. Nonetheless, many times, we are not strong enough to access that knowledge.

Your success is always your choice and we all have aspirations in life that drives us to do what we do every day. We are in school because we have a career aspiration that we want to achieve. We wake up early in the morning to go to work or do business because we need to have a better life in the future. We all have a future ahead of us, a past to be remembered, and today to make a difference. Never stagnate yourself for the past because you have today to make a difference. In the streets, you see lots of people on the move to different places without being forced or guided. Few who don't have anything to do sit on public benches.

A true warrior of success is the one who makes the best choices with a focus on achieving the impossibilities. Not accepting to be stopped by any circumstance is the power within. You have the power to change your life at any given moment.

What do We Require to Make Choices?

Knowledge – knowledge is the ability to understand what surrounds us by having all the right information we need at hand in order to make firm choices. The extent to which we familiarize ourselves with certain things influences our choices greatly. For instance, one may decide to choose a degree course at a certain university or college. After a year of study, discover many barriers that hinder career progression.

This can lead to regrets for having accepted to undertake the course.

In my first year in campus, I faced the same ordeal. Fellow students influenced me to change my course on the basis of its marketability. Since we do not have sufficient information about the courses as well as the employers' needs in the job market, we tend to be lured to change our courses. At one point I began to wonder if I had made the right choice. What if I had gone for economics? What if I had chosen some other university? What if I had pursued law? What if I had gone abroad?

A life full of regrets will lead to loss of hope and finally failing to achieve our goals and dreams.

Learn from the experience of others – experience, it is said, is the best teacher but most of us would not want to experience something painful to learn from it. Therefore, it's best if we always take time and learn from what other people have passed through and mostly engage our mentors or those people we admire to follow their footsteps in life. Learning from the experience of others will protect us from passing through tough moments while climbing the ladder of success. One of the wrong choices we can make in life is to give a deaf ear to any teaching we get from experienced people.

Seek guidance from mentors or elderly – a mentor or an elder can give us honest feedback about our performance. They caution us on what not to do, introduce us to invaluable connections, and give us advice about how to get to certain goals and dreams. The mentors and the elderly have been through the ups and downs of life. They got the full experience of what is ahead of us. Get advice from them to help you navigate through life's storms without getting yourself into trouble. It will save you from wasting lots of time trying to straighten your path. They can teach you how to change your life by emulating the hero we want to be.

Weigh options – take a good look at each side of a coin. Would you be better off with or without this person, thing or situation? What can it possibly bring to your life that will help you be more successful, happy, or healthy? Make two lists and write down the pros and cons of taking action and following a particular course. Again, be honest to yourself in order to shape your future. There are good and bad points in every situation. Which list is longer? Choose the better option that will build your present and future life.

Think long term – you need to stretch your imagination a bit in trying to look into the future. We often look into our short term situation and forget about our future. How many times have we complained about our present situation? For instance, the pain we had to endure to work hard in school, the sleepless nights to study well to pass our exams? How will it be if we had succumbed to the pleasure of the present? You may decide to miss classes and avoid stress all the time but risk ruining your future success.

The following questions will help out in identifying a proper choice in every situation:

- What are my options and what are the pros and cons of each option?
- A year from now, if I decide to do X, what might the choice look like? (This will help visualize the finish line, though we cannot predict the future.)
- What's the worst outcome?
- What would I tell a friend to do?
- Is this choice in line with my long term goals?
- What is the risk of not doing it?
- What does my experience or the experience of others tell me about the decision I am about to make?

Parenting as a Roadmap to Success

Parents are second after God because they play the role of God here on earth. They bring forth new-borns and ensure that they grow into responsible humans. Parents work hard and sacrifice for the good of their children. The parenting roles are crucial to their children's character development. The basic traditional roles of being a parent are to nurture and educate children, discipline them, manage the home and financially support the family. The main idea is that parents live for the best interests of their children. This will help them have a complete biological, social, psychological, and emotional growth. Parents made that best choice to bring us to this world; therefore respect to our parents is paramount and important. Thus, we should never forget that parents have a big responsibility—they mould their kids when they can't make sober and reasonable choices in their lives.

Parental Roles in Child Development

EDUCATION

In order to raise children properly, parental duties should not only be limited to food, shelter and protection but also require teachings that shape knowledge and character. This will prepare them to face the real world. To facilitate learning, a parent should have patience and understanding. The main goal here is to provide the children with the best education possible. A parent has to be a kin observer as well as an instructor so as to have an overview of their children's behaviours, moods, and activities. A parent who wants to be successful in teaching a child ought to be a model to that child. That is, a model to show the child how to be a good man or woman.

Ensuring that children are exposed to various opportunities that will help them grow into healthy members of the community is a crucial parenting role. To successfully integrate children into the community, parents should give them knowledge of their respective culture. Thus, they will have the necessary information and skills to grow up into an adapted adult. It is important to guide children towards social adaptation and integration. This will help kids develop appropriate coping skills in order to gain independence. Parents should also explain and carry out tasks with their children. Such tasks may include going through their books to ascertain what they learn in school as well as helping them with homework. Taking time to discuss with children what they did in school is part of community service which is a key parenting role in child education. It is not all about paying school fees and buying learning materials. This will help them learn how to make choices thus building their reasoning capacity.

PROVIDE GUIDANCE, DIRECTION, AND HELP

This role requires a kin listener who offers appropriate direction and guidance in the process of personal development and growth. The most effective way to help children is to advise them. This involves giving guidance in every step of child development without interrupting their work. Help them cope with the situation, but don't solve their problems as they need to find out solutions on their own. Give them a sense of direction and provide sufficient support to succeed and to feel that they are the source of the achievement. Step back and facilitate your children to gain independence by helping them handle and balance their needs.

As a parent, understand their need to be independent without losing all your authority. When children show a certain level of responsibility and independence, they extend their privileges and freedoms, but hold them back when their behaviour goes wrong. At an early stage parents make decisions for their children. At teenage, parents assist their children to decide and provide the wisdom to make the final decision on their own. Assist your child in the achievement of a task; help them only when necessary and only as far as needed.

Make sure you protect your children and warn them of the dangers of the world. Teach your child the difference between right and wrong, and how that wrong may be harmful both for them and for others. Your goal is to protect your children from dangers they may be vulnerable to in order to keep them safe. Children feel safe when there is continuity and consistency in daily routines. Furthermore, they feel safer when an atmosphere of love is created.

Familiarize your children with the diverse pros and cons, and benefits of the most relevant ways to make a living, but let them choose their own career. Ask various questions to get the child to discover exactly what it is they want to do or be.

SUPPORT AND MOTIVATE THE CHILD

If you want the child to be successful and to achieve his goals, encourage and motivate him. Positive motivation and encouragement is a must. Love your kids both when they succeed and when they fail. Provide empathic encouragement as a reward for an achievement, also to minimize the frustrations of failure. Teach the child to look at failure as a situation of learning and not as a tragic situation. Listen and be supportive, encourage instead of crushing the child's capacity to say no, at all costs. Motivate and persuade children to achieve more than they thought possible. Motivate the child and even push him to strive even harder, if you want him to gain a strong will.

Don't think that your children are sufficient to themselves and that they will grow up into strong young adults by themselves. Children should be personally motivated and trained to achieve their tasks. In short, you must be the personal coach of your kids. Be active and influence your kid's development. Praise your children when they achieve something and motivate them when they fail to achieve their goals.

Always Have Face-to-Face Communication With Your Child

Nowadays, you rarely find families having physical time together. All our attention has been diverted to our phones hence have less time with our children. You may find on one side a kid has a phone playing games and on the other side parents on their phones chatting. Phones have robbed and will continue robbing our children's future and dreams. We need to come out and take full charge all the time.

Children find friends and lots of people who are willing and are ready to communicate and give them the attention they lack at home on social media platforms. Facebook, Instagram, Snapchat, WhatsApp, and many others that are risky and they may be exposed to bad and obscene content, cyberbullies, fraud, and other risks they are oblivious of. Television might take the role of parental guidance from the programs aired.

Parents ought to take responsibility by giving guidance on what children should do while at home. Preparing a schedule of activities and monitoring what your child does while at home is being involved in their well-being. Limit their access to phones, Internet, and TV by having face-to-face communication from time to time in order to build a relationship with them.

Discipline Appropriately

A major aspect of the parent's role is to establish and maintain order in family by setting rules on what or not to be done. Understand what the child is communicating directly or indirectly by their attitudes and behaviours. Always respond consistently, appropriately, sensitively, and gently. Give corrective feedback to your child when their behaviour is inappropriate. An emphatic talk sometimes helps children become conscious of their mistakes. However, if they don't listen then the parent has to impose other punishments. Reacting angrily to a situation increases the tendency of a child to be defensive rather than accepting or looking into the problem. You have to do what is best for your children, rather than overlook their ways of behaving in order to meet your need for silence. Be firm and fair. Don't wait till things get out of hand. Deal with every issue immediately.

If your child is involved in an incidence of indiscipline either in school or community, avoid a defensive form of approach towards the case. Study the matter and get deep into it and discipline where needed. For example, in the incidence where a teacher or an elder has disciplined your child; ensure you don't get emotional and disrespect either the teacher or the elder in front of the child. Since children learn a lot from parents, the child may emulate your actions. They might continue disrespecting teachers and the elderly as long as they are not their real parents. Take note that parenting is communal and we all take responsibility for our children in our community.

Set boundaries and limits to control the children, impose ground rules and standards if you want to cultivate good will. Build your authority, take charge and when limits are transgressed, issue ultimatums, enforce discipline and impose consequences. Another parental duty is to encourage your children to keep time for every activity they do at home.

KNOW WHEN AND HOW TO GIVE FAVOURS AND FREEDOM

As a parent, know that the future success of your child is in your hands. You choose what to offer your child as they grow. You don't have to be too soft on your child, let the child know there are some things they can't access at a certain age. There was an incidence of a three-year-old child who disturbed the parents and brought mayhem when they were getting inside a mall. The child created a scene and people started focusing on the family. Some thought the kid was maybe being kidnapped. To their surprise, the mother finally took out a phone from the purse and gave the child. Suddenly, the child went silent and was happy. Imagine at that age a parent can succumb to the orders of a three year old child! What would happen as the child grows up? Parents need to take charge and utilize the power they have.

GUIDE YOUR CHILD INTO KNOWING GOD WELL

Our spiritual growth plays a great role in what we become in the future. In all the different religions, ensure the child is brought up knowing God and being prayerful. To accomplish these, parents should practice them at home. Show them how to pray by praying together at home and at the place of worship. Let them understand that God is the creator of the universe thus should always thank and respect Him for giving us the gift of life.

All this require adequate time, patience, and diligence. As a parent, take full responsibilities over your children. We should not be too much possessed with work or business to a point of neglecting our parenting responsibilities. Let's journey with them as they grow and start their God's purpose here on earth.

Finally, as a parent, you have to be strong and do your best for your children. Put your children's needs first. Be a giver rather than a receiver, give and go on giving. At the same time, demand to know the roles played by your child in order to be successful. Thus, they will excel in school academics, talents as well as respecting the family ground. You also have to continually learn, improve, and optimize your parenting knowledge and skills.

Attitude

One of our most important choices is the choice of our attitude. Do you realize that you, and only you, can choose your attitude? Attitude is how we respond positively or negatively towards a certain idea, person, or situation.

The attitude with which we approach life is a choice of every day. We have the power to choose the position or perspective we will assume toward specific events and people in our lives. The attitude we choose determines whether we scowl at each perceived flaw or welcome the challenge of the moment. Are we prepared to transform even the toughest conflict into an opportunity for growth?

Our attitude does not emerge from what happens to us but instead from how we decide to interpret what happens to us. Decide to adopt strong beliefs that create a good attitude rather than beliefs that create a bad attitude because this will determine how you interpret something and therefore your attitude.

If we believe we are inadequate, failures, undeserving of joy and happiness; then this is the negative reality we can expect to manifest and experience. Alternatively, when we see ourselves as adequate, valued and deserving, we are more likely to realize joy and fulfilment. Adopting a positive attitude in advance helps us overcome life's challenges.

Our attitude can influence our perceptions of scarcity or abundance. So, we can choose between the perception of ourselves as not smart enough, not likeable or good enough to deserve love and happiness or see ourselves as intelligent, capable and worthy of all the love and fulfilment we desire.

Rarely do we get to make all the choices regarding a situation. However, we invariably have an opportunity to play a role, make a contribution or influence the outcome. Our attitude affects the quality of that contribution. We have the power to support our experiences and interactions by having an open, flexible, and loving attitude. You can choose an attitude that will open your eyes to the valuable possibilities. You can choose an attitude that will attract success and accomplishment to you like a magnet. No matter what has happened in the past or where you are now, you are free to choose whatever attitude you wish.

Have an attitude of solving problems rather than seeing problems. Problem-solvers are the richest and most successful people in the world. Such people are ready to take on anything and no challenge is impossible. They have answers for seemingly difficult problems and do not get shaken by anything.

Attitude also determines how you relate with other people. Your relations with other people are one of the driving forces or factors in whether or not you are successful. People are drawn towards those with a positive, friendly, and inspiring attitude like bees to flowers. They want to work with them and for them. They easily get on board with any ideas the positive person has. Inversely, people distance themselves from those with self-defeating attitudes, making it all the more difficult for those with a poor attitude to find success.

Irrespective of how much you achieve in life, you will always feel unhappy if you constantly focus on what you don't have. Appreciate the things you have and never desire to live somebody's life, live your own life. Everybody is created differently and no one owns everything in the world. Our attitude is either our greatest asset or one of our greatest stumbling blocks. It's completely our choice and it's a choice we need to make every single day. Today is mine to make. Let me choose my attitude and future with care.

Note:

You don't die if you fall into water; you die only if you don't swim. Let's stop complaining and choose to change the situation. Many times we complain a lot about the situation around us than focusing on the solutions that will change the problem to opportunities. Building a positive attitude is like holding a powerful torch that lights your life.

Always Plan

Most of the time we are reminded that if one fails to plan, one plans to fail. Believe that in one way or another, you may have been confused and failed to plan well. Without proper planning, you risk sticking to the normal life schedule. Early planning enables you know what you want to do, when, and how to do it.

When you're young you might think you have all the time in the world, and then all of a sudden you have to start making important choices. What activities do I want to do? Which career should I join? Which subjects should I pick in school? Then you have to decide about further education, work, and careers. The major concern is that the choices we make along the way can affect the future we choose for ourselves. While our future can always be altered and is our own to choose, the journey can be made much easier by planning for the future you want today.

Proper planning is much needed to not only encourage us to achieve the goal we set out for ourselves, but also to break it up into simple goals that makes achievement much more tenable. Planning may not seem like it's an integral part of success but, once you yield its benefit, it'll prove important in every area of your life.

Planning gives us a clear perspective on what needs to be done, what goals are to be achieved, and what amount of time will be required to complete the said goals. It is highly relevant to say that planning can be closely associated with having proper time management. This encourages the planner to set aside a reasonable time for a specific task before moving ahead to the next. Self-imposed deadlines are a healthy form of motivation which is needed to overcome procrastinations.

Ensure you clearly outline your plan for your future goals and dreams you need to achieve. Finally, have a plan on how to achieve them.

2

The Power of Positive Thinking

What is Positive Thinking?

POSTIVE THINKING ENTAILS focusing on the bright side of a situation that will be beneficial to your vision and always having solutions to problems. Positive thinkers recognize both the bright side and the negative. They choose to focus their energy and time on the side that's going to promote the most positive outcome.

It is an individual's choice to live a happy and successful life and we always strive and work hard towards achieving it. Moreover, it all starts in your mind. Your beliefs shape your reality. Do you often invest in the energy of seeing things in a positive rather than a negative perspective? Do you believe in impossibility or possibility? Positive thinkers stress on achieving health, happiness, and success; they know where their strength lie, and they utilize their strengths properly.

When in a challenging situation, they know that they can overcome it. They believe that they can overcome any obstacle and difficulty, but positive thinking is not a concept that everyone believes and follows.

When you change your outlook towards life, everything falls into place. As the saying goes, life is ten percent of what happens to you and ninety percent of how you react to it. The power is in your hands. You are the only one who can change your life. Whenever you face a stressful situation, if you focus on your strength and put your best foot forward, you can turn the tables anytime. All you have to do is change the way you think. If you believe in yourself, you can overcome any hurdle. Never let others overpower you. If you are failing at something; take a deep breath and try to analyse the situation. Listen to constructive criticism only. All of this will help you to understand your strengths as well as your weaknesses. Then, use your strengths to win over your weaknesses. This, in turn, will help you to come up with a proper solution to your problem. Eventually, you will get what you want and enjoy a happy and successful life.

Pessimism is negative thinking. Life throws each of us obstacles. No one goes through life without challenges, or without running into obstacles. What's important is how you overcome obstacles. If life throws stones at you, collect the stones and use them to build a house. You can also decide to cry and lament over the pain and sufferings you got from being stoned. The choice is yours.

In life we experience several negative emotions like anger, guilt, anxiety, or sadness. That also means we get consumed by negative thoughts. Negative thoughts lead to worry and stress which eventually may lead to health problems. Habits like self-hate lead to a vicious cycle of self-doubt and low self-esteem. Guilt and low self-esteem will hold your life hostage. However, you can always choose to become better. A more positive version of yourself will transform your everyday life.

Ask yourself: being a prisoner of my past, maintaining the

status quo, or upholding my responsibilities, keeping alive hopes and dreams, what is the wise thing to do? When you answer that question in a positive way, your hopes will not be cut short and you will have a bright future.

I believe that you cannot be both a victim and a victor at the same time, choose to be one or the other. Be a positive thinker!

How to be a Positive Thinker

Focus on What You Want to Become in the Future

If you really want something, focus on it. This is the best way to become a positive thinker. Take your focus away from what you don't want, and spend more time thinking about what you want. It might take some conscious effort, especially in the beginning. Eventually, you will spend more time visualizing and focusing on what you want. You'll start to see it happening!

Focusing is all about positive energy and replaying the story that you wish to see in your mind. The Greek philosopher and scientist, Aristotle, said:

"

First, have a definite, clear, practical ideal; a goal or an objective. Second, have the necessary means to achieve your ends: wisdom, money, materials, and methods. Third, adjust all your means to that end.

"

Express Gratitude for Every Good Thing in Your Life

Be grateful for what you have. It is easy to focus on what is going wrong instead of what is going right. I truly believe and know that people who appreciate what they have are healthier, happier, and more effective. Throughout the day, look for things to be thankful for.

Read And Memorise Inspiring Words

Draw inspiration from the sayings of great minds like William Shakespeare, Albert Einstein, Abraham Lincoln, Norman Vincent Peale, Barrack Obama, Nelson Mandela, Martin Luther King Junior, Confucius, just to mention but a few. Find people who inspire you the most and draw inspiration from their lives/sayings. This is a powerful way to immensely change your outlook on life. You could get the quotes printed and placed on walls in your house/room, office, diary, or desk. This always inspires you as well as other people who visit that place.

Read Motivational Books

Read books that will open your mind and motivate you, books that will make you appreciate and value yourself as well as empower and inspire you to grow and do more. Motivational literature is fuel to rejuvenate your energy into productivity.

An inspiring book, *Beyond Limits* by Pepe Minambo, taught me that human beings have no limits. We can conquer the world or if you ran fast enough, you could fly. It is reflective, and it taught me that my dreams of becoming the president of Kenya are valid; that it's possible as long as I dare to dream bigger and live a more fulfilling life. Motivational books ignite our imagination.

George R R Martin, the brain behind the *Game of Thrones*

books-turned-TV series, wrote that a man who reads lives a thousand lives while a man who doesn't read lives only one life.

After reading *Beyond Limits,* I started making a journey of inspiring others in my writing and motivational talks.

Create Personal Affirmations and Restate Them Everyday

Always be cognizant of what you say. Every word we speak is an affirmation. If we focus on the positive, we can change and influence our perception of reality. The tongue is powerful and what we say is an affirmation of what we may or may not become.

Meditation

Meditation is not just for spirituality. Meditation can bring peace, tranquillity, and consciousness in your busy life. It helps us interact more with our inner consciousness to figure out more about the energy we release. Meditation helps us have time to reflect on our achievements and failures as well.

Be Around Positive People

You are the company you keep. If you hang around and interact with negative people, you will be filled with negativity. On the other hand, if you surround yourself with positive people you become exposed to positive values and ideals while reinforcing and strengthening your positive mental attitude. This is why it is so important to be keen on the people you surround yourself with and even more so the frequency and the length of time you spend with them. Support from fellow human beings is one of the biggest forms of encouragement. When you surround yourself with positive people, you increase your chances of success.

Have a Hobby or Passion

Remember to have fun and enjoy yourself because that's the secret to a happy life and a better you. Put work and obligations aside once in a while and do something that you love and are passionate about, be it swimming, physical exercise, reading, or watching movies. It will do you good in putting your energy into positivity. When you are passionate about what you do, everything else in your life changes for the better. All work and no play makes Jack a dull boy.

"

Often people ask how I manage to be happy despite having no arms and legs. The quick answer I give is that I have a choice. I can be angry about not having limbs or I can be thankful that I have a purpose. I chose gratitude.

"

Nick Vujicic

3

The Power of Desire

Desire Is The burning itch that pushes you to choose to do what you do. Desire come to people with an insatiable need for action. If you have sufficient desire to succeed, nothing can stop you from becoming a winner, a leader, or an achiever.

Look around and see the effects of desire in every human act, good or bad. Every deed that we do, good or bad, is prompted by desire. One is kind because they desire to be kind; being kind satisfies them, while another is cruel from precisely the same kind of motive. One person does their duty well because they desire to do it; it satisfies them. Desire is the motivating power behind all actions.

You don't act on every desire but upon the strongest desire or the average of your strongest desires. This average of desires is that which constitutes your nature or character. You are not supposed to be a slave of your desires because you can control, regulate, govern, and guide them in any direction that is good for your future.

When you desire something, it means that thing is of great value to you. It is something that will bring you happiness, joy, peace, and satisfaction if attained. I love what the Bible says about desire in Proverbs 13:19: A desire accomplished is sweet to the soul.

Desire is the starting point of all achievements, not a hope, not a wish, but a keen pulsating desire which transcends everything.

Napoleon Hill

If you anxiously want something, you'll make it happen whether good or bad. However, if you don't want something, even the best of strategies won't serve. Desire has an element of force in it, it compels you to come out of your comfort zone and take action. When you desire a thing, you think out of the box. Your mind explores how that thing can be achieved. Desire leads to planning and then action.

Unfortunately, most people incorrectly seek strategies on how to succeed. In this way, they put the cart before the horse. The right strategy will show itself when you are clear about what you want. So, how do you know what you want? Most people are waiting for an epiphany, or someone or something outside of them to rattle or shake them. Or, they just want a quick fix. Hence, the focus on strategy and not on vision and values. Nothing can stop you once you decide what you want. But you have to decide. To quote Napoleon

Hill, *there is one quality which one must possess to win, and that is definiteness of purpose, the knowledge of what one wants, and a burning desire to possess it.*

If you're waiting for something to wake you up so you finally have the passion, motivation, or desire to put your whole soul into life, you'll be waiting a long time. Rather than waiting, your only chance to full living is to proactively do something on your own. When was the last time you really tried to do something? If you're like most people, you're probably putting half-thought and half-effort into most of what you're doing and thus delivering you half results or sometimes failure therefore not achieving the best out of yourself. Give it all your best in what you do and you will achieve more.

There is nothing like the next opportunity. Every day as we wake up, new opportunities present themselves. The one you have at hand is the opportunity, actualize it. However, we sometimes spend too much time trying to perfect something before we do it. There is nothing like perfection in life. Instead of waiting for perfection, run with what you got and give it your best, and fix it along the way.

Finally, be focused and desire to do better and better each day as it brings new opportunities.

A young man once approached Socrates and asked the philosopher how he could acquire wisdom and knowledge.

"Follow me," Socrates said in response, as he led the young man down to the sea. The young man followed as Socrates began wading through the water, first at the ankle, then knee, then waist, and finally to shoulder height.

Then, rather abruptly, Socrates grabbed the young man and dunked him under the water. The young man struggled desperately and just before he blacked-out, Socrates pulled him up.

Infuriated, the young man screamed, "What are you doing?! Trying to kill me?"

Calmly, Socrates responded, "Absolutely not. If that was my intention, I would not have pulled you up."

"Then why did you just do that?" the young man gasped.

"When you want wisdom and insight as badly as you desired that breathe of air, then you shall have it," Socrates replied while looking directly into his eyes. Then, he turned to the shore and walked away.

4

The Power of Now

I**F** I**T'S** N**OT** the right time to begin, then when? I bet the right time to begin was last year, but a year later, you still think it's not the right time to begin. Look at your life. Can where you are now be compared to where you could be?

"

The best time to plant a tree was 20 years ago.
The second best time is now.

"

Chinese Proverb.

There is never a right time to begin, now is the time. It will never be convenient to be and live how you know you desire to. If it was convenient, everyone would be living at a much higher level than they are. There would be no internal conflict. Instead, most people wait for someone or something outside of them to wake them from their apathy or pick them. It's not going to happen for those people. We are constantly on the move. However, the best time to plan and actualize your future to reality is now.

If you want something, you have to want it as bad as you want air. And you have to start NOW. If you are waiting for the perfect moment such as when you clear the busy schedule or when your motivation is sky-high to be ready to start, then you are going to be waiting for a long time.

There is so much in your life right now that is worth living for. You have people in your life right now that you're taking for granted. You have an endless well of untapped potential within you. Life doesn't stop and wait for you to get on the train. It's always moving and you need to jump on. What is the difference between the preferred time and now? The sun rises and sets down at the same time every day. So why wait until the preferred time to act? Every day that you wake up and put your feet on the floor is a new beginning. Stop procrastinating and act now.

There is no next opportunity, only the one right in front of you. When are you going to start living? Nothing can stop you once you decide what you want. But you have to decide. The seeds you are planting today will sprout for your future self. The mess you make today, your future self will have to clean. Everything you do now is an investment in your life and the greatness of your future.

The past is the blueprint of our present. We may have regretted our past and feel like we need the best for our future. Thus, we need to focus on what we do today. When we focus on the present we focus on the task at hand. We give our all to what we are doing and we determine the outcomes.

Seizing each moment in life allows us to prolong its value and make it more meaningful. When we live in the moment we enjoy and savour every minute. We don't sacrifice quality for quantity. Of course, this doesn't mean we don't need to plan, set goals or prepare for the future. We can do all of these things and still enjoy each moment as it unfolds.

For instance, if you set a goal to exercise each day, you would carry on with it while enjoying every bit of it. If you train yourself to live in each moment, you immerse yourself in it and begin to discover its beauty and wonder. You focus and manage your energy. Professional athletes understand and employ this kind of focus well. To make every moment, count you must embrace it. Everything you do and every person you come in contact with deserves your full attention. Even when resting, you should savour the moment. It allows you to recharge, refresh, and gain clarity.

Quite often, we have high expectations of ourselves and our lives. We rush things without enjoying the moment. What's the rush? Where do we think we're going? If you don't stop and think about where you're at, you'll probably miss out on the important things in life. Instead, when you appreciate each moment and learn from the experiences, you live consciously, purposefully, and responsibly. Likewise, when you live in the past and don't let go of painful experiences, perceived wrongs, or difficult times, you condemn yourself to a present and future of the same. We cannot change the past. We can, however, come to terms with it, know that it's over, and move on.

Live in the present, now.

Imagine you had a bank account that deposited 86,400 shillings each morning. The account carries over no balance from the previous to the next day. It never allows you to keep cash balance. Every evening it cancels whatever part of the amount you had failed to use during the day. What would you do? Draw out every shilling each day.

We all have such a bank. Its name is time. Every morning, it credits you with 86,400 seconds. Every night it writes off as lost, the time you have failed to use wisely. It carries over no balance to the following day. It allows no overdraft so you can't borrow against yourself or use more time than you have. Each day, the account starts afresh. If you fail to use the day's deposits, it's your loss and you can't appeal to get it back.

There is never any borrowing time. You can't take a loan out on your time or against someone else's. The time you have is the time you have and that is it. There is no going back. There is no drawing against tomorrow. Therefore, there is nothing like inadequate or too much time. Time management is yours to decide how you spend time; just the way you decide how you spend the money. It is never the case of us not having enough time to do things, but the case of whether we want to do them and where they fall in our priorities."

5

The Power of Determination

DETERMINATION MEANS FIRMNESS of purpose or intention. It is the strength of your will and focus to remain steadfast in your effort. It means having the ability to stay on course. Remain focused on your goals. Stand up to problems and obstacles with conviction. Stay fixed and firm about your decisions, solutions, and intentions. Apply the power of your will to your dreams and desires with resolve, grit, fortitude, faith, and courage.

If there is one gift that you can give to yourself in life is to be what you want to be, the power of determination. Without determination you are a passive spectator of your life. Determination is the one quality in life that makes a difference between a winner and a loser or a leader and a follower. Without it, your dreams are wild with no meaning in life. If you have determination, nothing can distract you from fulfilling your goals to realize your dreams.

Taking action is essential if you want to achieve your goals, dreams, and desires. To ensure that you stay in action, persistence is key.

During your journey to success, you will encounter roadblocks, hardships, and challenges. There will be times when you will want to quit, give up, and go back to doing something else. Obstacles will obstruct your progress, delay your success, disturb you, and may even mislead you, but they cannot withstand the power of determination. It is the power that you generate within yourself to remain true to your cause and conviction, and march towards your achieving your goals.

Determination is a strong and valuable resource in itself. If you have it, you can aim for the stars. You are successful or unsuccessful to the extent you are determined and committed. With determination, we can accomplish many goals in our lives. With faith in God and confidence in yourself, and with strong determination, you can achieve the impossible. Moreover, realize the most difficult dreams and achieve excellence and incredible success in your life. It is the one quality that will guarantee you success. It will ensure you have the willingness to stick with it, to see it through to the end, as well as refuse to settle for anything less than your dream.

Before you take up any project or goal, you should know whether you have the determination to stick to your plans and reach your goals. Your determination has to arise from within and derive its reinforcement from your thinking and beliefs rather than circumstances. Only then will you be able to sustain your effort, even when the going gets tough. Determination is your inner strength. Like the hardwood inside a tree, it gives you the power to stand tall and face the winds of turmoil. The following factors strengthen your resolutions:

- faith in yourself and God,
- clear goals,
- knowledge and skills,
- self-esteem,
- positive mental attitude,
- courage,
- self-motivation,
- visualizing the end,
- positive self-affirmations,
- supporting people, and
- empowering thoughts and beliefs.

With determination, you can scale any mountain of fear and doubts you may have; you can find your way through the most difficult situations. Determination does not mean you will be insensitive to the reality of the situation, but being adaptable and flexible to all life situations. A determined person is not interested in being tough for toughness sake, but to overcome obstacles and reach their goals. Hence, they remain open-minded about possibilities and opportunities, but firm in their commitment and convictions. Discipline and determination go hand in hand. If you have them, you become unstoppable.

Be Ready to Pay the Price

Everything in life is worth paying for; all we need is the key to unleash our potentials. That key is passion and persistence to work for whatever we desire in life. However, before you can choose to pay the price, you must know what the price is before working on it. If you don't know what will truly be required to make your dreams a reality, investigate. Research the costs other people have had to pay to achieve dreams similar to yours. You may even want to interview these individuals to discover the sacrifices they had to make along the way.

You may find that some costs are more than you want to pay. Only you can decide what is right for you and what price you are willing to pay.

But if the price is something you are willing to pay, commit yourself to achieve your dream, no matter what it takes. The willingness to do whatever is required is the magic ingredient that helps you persevere in the face of adversity, even personal injury.

Achieving goals and dreams requires sacrifice. It might mean putting everything in life on hold in favour of working toward your dreams; investing all of your savings; or giving up a few hours of sleep each night. Many people proclaim to want to achieve their goals, yet are unwilling to pay the price.

No matter how well you plan and how well you execute your plan, you are bound to be disappointed, derailed, or fail along the way.Adversity allows you to be resilient. Whenever you confront an obstacle or run into a roadblock: go around it, over it, or through it. No matter how hard it seems, the longer you persist, the more likely you will succeed.

Determination is the energizer of life. Determined people do not look back when in pursuit of their goals. They may make mistakes but they don't quit. They learn from their mistakes and get on with life until they succeed. They believe that the power of determination can make them reach their goals, no matter the setbacks. They are always optimistic. They believe things are possible for them. Look at the success stories of people, who have chalked up success in their chosen fields—they all had the spirit of determination. That is the attitude you should hold on to.

6

The Power of Yes and No

THE POWER OF "Yes" is simply seeing and engaging with opportunities that we are presented with. The power of "Yes" is critical because it keeps us moving forward. Not engaging in the 'Power of Yes' we can become stagnant and stall our progress. The 'Power of Yes' enables us to open more great opportunities. But sometimes we have to note that we easily say yes to things. That has been our habit and what we love, yet, get it hard to new changes.

Successful people know that to accomplish their goals, they will have to say 'no' to certain tasks, activities, and demands. This could be from their friends, family, and colleagues. In short-term, you might sacrifice a bit of instant gratification, but when your goals come to fruition, it will all be worth it. We tend to think of the word "no" as a bad thing.

> **"**
>
> He who would accomplish little must sacrifice little; he who would achieve much must sacrifice much; he who would attain highly must sacrifice greatly.
>
> **"**

James Allen

We're taught to say yes, to keep our minds open to new opportunities and to chase the next shiny thing that is dangled in front of us. Some things that have been great in your life have been successful just because you said yes to them. Yet, success in history shows us that "no" is the more powerful word.

"No" works because it enables you to maintain your focus on one or two things that are truly important to you. It works because it allows you to see things through until completion. It works because when you say "yes" to one thing, you're saying "no" to absolutely everything else.

Most people are stuck in obligations they don't even like, because they didn't dare to say no. As a result, their days are spent doing things they don't like that suck precious time and energy that could be spent on building their legacy. You need to say "no" to such duties.

To get into that 'really successful people' category, you need to set your priority. Notice I said 'priority' rather than 'priorities'. If you have more than one priority, you aren't prioritizing anything. Everybody has one thing that works overtime for them, where 20 percent of the actions they take yield 80 percent of the results. That one thing needs to be your priority.

When you say yes to the 'kinder-good' opportunities; the ones that make you say things like, 'sure that could be fun,' or 'alright that sounds interesting', you forfeit your chance to say yes to amazing opportunities.

Your life's legacy requires your best work and a lot of time to do it. You can't create a legacy if you're always distracted with good-not-great opportunities, even if you're making a few extra bucks. Life is about making the best choices that can help you and the people around you live a better life. However, these choices are not always easy to make. A decision made might, for instance, have great short term value, but hurts you or others in the long term. Thus, my hope is that by understanding the value of saying both yes and no will help you make more effective decisions moving forward.

Stories abound of men and women who took the challenge that afterwards rewarded them. Wangari Maathai, an environmentalist, relentlessly fought for women's liberation and environmental conservation. Wangari was the first woman in East and Central Africa to earn a doctoral degree. From her Green Belt Movement, which she founded in 1977, she planted over 45 million trees around Kenya. Ultimately, she won the Nobel Peace Prize in 2004. Through her actions (including problems dealing with police brutality), even braving the police, she rose to international recognition.

I once accepted a challenge to participate in an East and Central Africa community service competition. I ultimately became among the eight Kenyan youth to represent Kenya in the summit which was held in Uganda. During the summit, I met and had an engaging conversation with Madam Graca Machel, wife to South African icon Nelson Mandela. A yes and no in life will build or destroy you, always have the best yes and no in any situation.

7

The Power of Focus

>

Turn your face toward the sun and the shadows will fall behind you.

>

Maori Proverb

YOU CANNOT AVOID problems in life. No sooner is one solved than another crops up. But don't dwell on the problem. Focus on the end state and opportunities ahead. When you focus on problems, you will have more problems. When you focus on possibilities, you will have more opportunities.

When travelling from point A to point B, it's easy to be distracted. It takes discipline not to fall for the distractions.

We need to direct our minds into the light. Focusing on an illness will never create health. Focusing on unpaid school fees will not create abundance. Focusing our attention on a problem will only serve to magnify it.

Photography is an amazing way to learn about focus. This is because the very act of viewing life through the lens of a camera can help us develop a truly empowering skill. As you undertake a task, ask yourself how is your power of focus or were you distracted by small things around you? The more you focus on things that are destined to better your future and your vision, the more successful you will be in whatever you undertake.

My father always uttered the word 'focus' in all his pieces of advice to me. He was a soldier and he used to tell me that 'focus' in the military was important in everything. During parade and war, focus was the order of the day. When you don't focus you become prone to failure and confusion, and ultimately cost yourself.

Your attention is your biggest asset. It's important to keep it where it's supposed to be on the task at hand, which is, getting you one step closer to achieving your goals and dreams. So much is going on around us at any moment though it can be difficult to concentrate on the one activity, task, or even person, in front of us.

Knowing how to focus is crucial; especially today, as we live in the era of distraction. Obstacles will still come in the form of temptations, distractions (such as social media, messages, and television) as well the hundreds of thoughts on your mind at any given minute. You should eliminate all these to focus.

However, it doesn't seem to work like that. Generally speaking, it gets harder and harder to concentrate on what really matters as we constantly get overwhelmed due to loads of information rocketing our way. This information overload also makes us anxious and then we find all types of excuses to procrastinate.

What You Need to Sharpen Your Focus

Keep the Vision/Goals in Mind

Why do you even need to focus? Do you want to be the best student, the best business person, the best employee, the best employer? Think about it, knowing what you need to stay focused on can help us push through the tough and tedious part of accomplishing our goals. That's when our ability to focus is tested and when it's most needed.

Avoid Having Chaotic Days by Focusing on Important Tasks

If you have twenty tasks that need to be done every day, how effective do you think your focus will be? You can't expect to do those things with sophistication if you are too scatter-brained to focus. You need to break it down to the essentials.

Focus on only doing important tasks a day, but not everything. It is all you need to take steps towards accomplishing your goals. By doing one task at a time, you will find fast progress that will eventually lead you to do things.

Have Deadlines

Deadlines are essential while focusing. They keep your mind from wandering around. A deadline ensures you are focused fully into the task. When writing this book and many other books I have written, I have always given myself timelines. They usually guide me to give my mind, time, and energy into finishing it within the stipulated time. In this, you will find accomplishing your task on time and without hurry or mistakes.

That is why examinations are timed. This helps us focus on one goal and to finish the task in the right way.

Remove External Distractions

Ensure you always keep away from things that distract you. Is the television a distraction? Work in another room. Are the kids distracting you? Get up earlier and work before they wake up. Get to know how you deal with your distractions and on good time. Distraction pulls you back without you noticing. With distractions, you will lose focus of what you will be doing and use more energy and time on the task.

What you focus on expands. We all have the same number of hours each day. What are you expanding? Where are you directing your energy, your thoughts, your actions and ultimately your life?

8

The Power of Confidence

CONFIDENCE IS BELIEVING in yourself and believing in your abilities. With confidence, you feel on top, in power, and in control of everything in your life. It is a feeling in which you enjoy what you do. For instance, a athletes' confidence gives them a drive that pushes them to train harder, longer, and better.

How is it like to go about life without confidence? No matter what you do, you're not good enough. No matter how hard you train, you won't play well enough. No matter how hard you study, you feel like you're still going to fail. Your thoughts feel sluggish and you can't focus. Your mind is in shambles because you know that you can do better, but for some reason, it's just not clicking.

Your level of confidence determines your performance in the game, in the classroom, and in life. And the confidence you have for something that can determine so much to you is fragile. It is a fleeting thing that can last for months or only for a second.

I have struggled with confidence in most aspects of my life especially when I began writing books; it gave me sleepless nights. I could not believe in anything I did since I believed there are best writers out there and why should I get into a field I will be shamed? Afterwards, I found that it was entirely my fault to undermine my capability. I was the one who allowed self-doubt. I allowed my fears to change my personality and my anxieties to fuel my drive into negativity. But, I changed gears and built my confidence. I believed in learning more through believing in my capabilities and acting on them.

Despite the overwhelming presence of unfavourable factors, you must remember that you control your level of confidence. Sometimes we allow the world to persuade us to believe that our level of accomplishments is equivalent to who we are as a person. The truth is we can't sacrifice our self-esteem to please others. You cannot control what other people think of you or what you have accomplished. You also can't control the ill-fated events that occasionally occur in your life, but you can choose when and what you succumb to.

How to Build and Develop Confidence

Use Your Passion to Get You Through

Whenever in doubt, instead of remaining lost, think about something you are passionate about. What lights you up? What makes your heart shine? Finding something to inspire you can help push you through and reach your inner confidence. Even in difficult moments, pausing for just a moment to think of your passion can help you transfer those feelings of confidence and power.

Accept What You are Feeling and Move Past It

We are tested daily in all aspect but we have to see things through. Your aim should be to do your best, but no matter how hard we try, sometimes it just doesn't work out the way you envisioned it. Instead of feeling bad about it not working out and giving up; accept that even though it may not seem so, there is a bigger picture; a light at the end of the tunnel. We simply cannot see yet, and when we see it or the real reason, the bigger picture will reveal itself.

The difference is how you look beyond failure and how it affects you. Learn from it as you endeavour to do better because it really builds your confidence. Understand that those moments are stepping-stones. Using them to better yourself will help you move to a place where you feel comfortable by letting your confidence manifest itself.

Face Your Fears and Act

Fear is one of the worst enemies of success. When fear wraps its tentacles around you and keeps you in bondage, you will never be able to achieve your dreams. You must confront your fears, see them for what they are, toss them to the side, and pursue your dreams with relentless passion. Conquering fear and stepping forward to reach new lands and new ideas is what makes success possible. What are you afraid of today? What fear must you conquer to be able to achieve your dream? When you realize what it is, take an action that is diametric to that which you fear. This will confront and conquer the fear by giving you the first step in the right direction. After winning your fears, you gradually boost your confidence in all aspect.

Surround Yourself with Confident People

Always mingle with people who equally make your daily engagements equal to you. If you interact with people who have no confidence in their life, you will probably be affected and be infected to look down on yourself. Have people who motivate and see greatness in you even when you look down on yourself. You will always work to improve each other's confidence. Human beings tend to have a high affinity to motivation and support from people close to them.

9

The Power of Networking

No One Is an island in this world; harness the power of networking. When you meet someone who could help make your future bright, what do you do? As young people in the twenty-first century, we like taking photos whenever we meet prominent people. We forget to interact on how we can establish good relationships that would help us achieve our dreams/goals. Invest in constructive conversations. Avoid the distraction from your phone that will bar you from having that constructive conversation.

I have networked with a lot of people. I remember an interaction with my trainer in one of our activities immediately after completing my secondary school exams. I won the trainer's trust through how I engaged responsibly in my line of duty. After joining campus to pursue my bachelor's degree in maritime management, she once interacted with someone who had his own company in the maritime industry and through this, I was connected with him as my mentor. To date the relationship is strong and still on. I managed to have my internship at his place for eight months and in this, I gained a lot of knowledge and more networks in my career path. Don't always wait till you are done with studies to connect to the job market. The power is in your hands to interact and network to build that professional relationship that will be helpful to your career.

I came to realize that irrespective of your level of studies or the degrees you have; you have to frequently focus on widening your network. Without that, you will tarmac a lot trying to find your space into a successful life. The rate at which professionalized and educated young people are unemployed is widely attributed to lack or poor networking skills. Even though networking is necessary in terms of building your profession, it does not assure you of better relationship with those you network with. You need to offer more in showing off your unique skills to create your own space and career path.

The more you network the more links for opportunities open up. I have personally heavily relied on my circle of friends. I have not only found internship through connections but also been able to get feedback and help on any strategic plan I choose to work on. Likewise, I have shared opportunities, referred people, and offered advice to others. This doesn't mean we spend all our free time at said networking events, but always try to take advantage of natural opportunities to connect with people and develop meaningful relationships.

Remember networking is the shortcut to success but it helps build long term relationships. Building more healthy relationships and expanding your social circle and network will open new doors for you. It will also add value to your personal and professional life. You never know who you will be able to connect with and where that connection will lead.

Career and life advancement are as much about whom you know as what you know. That's exactly why being an effective networker is so important.

Networking can be a powerful tool. It can enhance your ability to lead and influence other people. However, this will happen only when the people in your network value your connection. They should value you for more than just being one of the hundreds of people in their network. The power of networking lies in how well the people you're networking with know you, how much they trust you, how much they gain from having you in their network, how frequently you communicate with them, and how many other powerful people exist in your network.

If you want to build an effective network, you must focus on what you can do for other people, not what they can offer you. This is the only way to build real and lasting relationships. The help you provide others defines your impact and your life. The relationships you build germinate and grow over the years. They come back to help you in unexpected, often life-changing ways.

Tips to Good Networking

Give Before You Receive It

One of the biggest networking mistakes people make is jumping the gun when asking for a favour. One cardinal rule of successful networking is: Give before you can get. Don't engage on the gear of requesting favours either financially or material things. I suppose even when you feel things are not going on well on your side, don't quickly rush to your networks to sort your issues out. At first focus on building friendship before they see you as a liability to them. Make them feel that they can rely on you as well that means you must be useful to their needs in some way.

Build Trust and Be Responsible

One will only get to connect to you well when indeed there is trust built in the friendship. Trust is not a one-day event and it takes longer to be trusted; with gradual engagement, you can build it. Are you reliable? Are you demonstrating competence? Are you helpful? Are you sincere? All these four components contribute to building a sense of trust and loyalty. Thus, this will be the bedrock of a strong network.

When I trust you, it makes it easier for me to deal with the increased risk that comes from lowering my guard. When I trust you, I open myself so that it's easier for us to collaborate. I tell you what I'm thinking, set aside formality and shift my focus from figuring out your intentions to getting work done together.

Have Value and Uniqueness in What You Engage On

Ensure that you do something great with your life as an individual. Your networks would want to know your value and would like to network with someone who has advanced at a personal level. What unique thing are you doing to increase your value? Our personality is built on what we consistently do.

10

The Power of Patience

Patience Is The ability to tolerate waiting and delays without becoming frustrated or agitated; or the ability to remain calm when facing difficulties and adversity.

Have you ever wondered why some people can tolerate anything that happens in their world and yet you can't seem to handle even the smallest of disruptions? Today's world is a *need it right now world*. Emails, text messages, and smartphones have made us much more accessible and our level of accountability much higher. The expectations for immediate attention are overwhelming and can negatively impact our productivity and patience. Patience also improves productivity because it creates a better and clearer state of mind for better decision making.

"

The key to everything is patience. You get
the chicken by hatching the egg, not by
smashing."

Paul J. Mayer

You have to set big and audacious goals to do great things. But setting the goals themselves is only the first part of the equation. If you want to do anything great, you have to learn the art of following through. It takes tenacity to follow through on our goals. You need the audacity to set a huge scary goal down and tell the world you're going to achieve it no matter what. It takes guts to claim a piece of the pie for your own. It can take years of waiting, or even a decade of gruelling work before you start to reap big results from all the hard work you've put in. It can be frustrating.

Learn the art of patience. Remember, Rome was not built in a day. The heights reached and kept by great people were not attained by sudden flight. So, do not expect to reach the top in one big leap.

No matter what your aspirations are, they must be achieved step by step. It is the steady constant drive towards your, goal not the speed with which you travel that will make your victory sure. Do something else while you wait and all will be well. Do you want to flatten a mountain? Start by carrying away small stones.

People who can exercise a certain degree of calmness and understanding when faced with difficult as well as stressful situations, seem to have a higher level of affinity to success. It seems like they can succeed more easily because they're able to keep their wits about them in tough times instead of getting all frustrated and angry. Essentially, they're able to keep their minds when the rest of us are ready to pull our hair out and scream at the top of our lungs. Too often what you think is what you fear the most. When a particular event or situation is off in the distance, we tend to assume the worst. We assume things will not work according to plan or we will be disappointed with the results.

Assumptions lead to impatience because the lack of knowledge and uncertainty can make you uncomfortable. Instead, consider the facts. Scrutinize to see if there is any history that can tell you what has happened in the past to provide assurances for the future.

To gain patience, you have to know what makes you impatient. What is it about the situation or person that is sending you over the edge? This may require you digging below the surface to find out what exactly it is that is getting under your skin.

People may remind you of someone else that you're not particularly fond of. Perhaps you are strapped on time and feel like you're not accomplishing what you intended to accomplish. Whatever it is that is bothering you, you need to give it a name and recognize it. You can't deal with something you don't understand.

Everything in life is a marathon, not a sprint, and you need 10,000 hours to be great. Who wouldn't want things to work out fast? However, even when looking down the vast tunnel where the light at the end signifies your future success, you still wonder why despite your best efforts it's just not happening for you. It's only human to wonder and beat ourselves up for not being successful yet. Whatever you are up to in life, you need patience to move in that tunnel to success. It all takes time and it's our greatest asset in life.

The problem with being patient is we don't think we have enough time. Time has become as much a commodity as gasoline. We can't get enough of it. We need more of it. We are constantly depleted of it. We are trying to do so much every day that we have no time left to be patient. We need to always plan to use that God-given time well.

However, sometimes things happen outside our control that impact our schedules and change our plans. We try not to think about the potential of such events until they actually happen. We don't make contingencies, instead limit our time by developing more ironclad schedules. But think about this for a minute: you can help relieve some of your impatience if you don't schedule yourself so tightly ... If you leave a little room for the unforeseen, so that, when they do occur, you have some room to adjust. At times things will happen that change your plans ... don't be surprised by them, expect them.

Artwork cannot be rushed and patience cannot be lost if the picture is to be finished. In any case, patience can't be easily acquired; you need to practice it over time.

11

The Power of Consistency

CONSISTENCY IS ABOUT building empowering habits and rituals that you partake in every single day. This will keep you focused on your highest priorities and goals while focusing on your long term dream. It is the ability to hold yourself accountable for the daily choices you make with no excuses and complaints. You and you alone are accountable for what you do or fail to do. All choices lie solely in your hands.

To be consistent means to concentrate on the present moment while maintaining a long term view. It will help you measure your results and the impact of your daily actions. With this regular feedback in your hands, you are better and knowledgeable about your failures and mistakes to help you effectively alter your course of action where required.

Think of something that you can't stop doing now. What

probably could have caused that? Consistency leads to habits. Habits form the actions we take every day. Consistency is necessary in life for you to succeed because anytime you begin anything new there is usually that excitement that keeps you motivated for weeks or even months. Eventually, that will wear off but with consistency, it will keep you going for long even after the early excitement.

Consistency is therefore all about repetition. It's about repeating the same actions (habits and rituals) over and over again. Gaining feedback from these actions and adjusting them accordingly to help you stay on track as you work towards your goal. And that, in essence, is the difference between success and failure in any field of endeavour and the key to high levels of achievement.

To be consistent means to fully dedicate your thoughts and energy completely to a task, activity or goal. That means staying engaged without distraction. It requires determination on your part and that you commit yourself to a sustained effort of action over the long term. What this essentially means is that you keep your word to yourself and others. That you will follow through with what you set out to do consistently over a period of time up until the moment your objectives are achieved. As such, consistency is all about your ability to be dependable, reliable, and responsible for all your choices, decisions, and actions.

Consistently doing the right things leads to amazing results. How can you know what the right things are? Find someone who's doing what you want to do and model them. Have you ever felt that you keep repeating the same negative habits that hinder you from achieving success? If you want to achieve anything of value and meaning in your life, you need to be consistent in them over the long-term and avoid or stop negative habits that ruin your future as Tony Robbins said: In essence, if we want to direct our lives, we must take control of our consistent actions. It's not what we do once in a while that shapes our lives, but what we do consistently.

Consistency builds momentum. For example, think about one of your goals. It requires consistent efforts to push toward that goal. If you are not consistently focused on achieving it, you will likely fall back into old habits or lose interest. Being consistent is the difference between failure and success. The power of consistency over time is reflected in your ability to fall in love with the process. It is not merely focusing on the result. Find ways to associate pleasure with activities that bring you closer to where you want to be in life.

Do you wonder why some people are trusted more than you, even when they are wrong? It's because consistency builds trust. Thus someone knows that you can be counted on to carry out a task or deliver a certain level of work when tasked. People often pay as much attention to your actions as to what you say. If you say you're going to do something, you have to do it. Imagine a supervisor who is friendly and joking one day, then the next day is angry and withdrawn, and another day is serious and reserved. People will develop a sense of uncertainty about him and begin to question his consistency. While none of us is 100% consistent, we must regularly assess if we are consistent enough in our words, actions, and performance to ensure a reasonable level of trust. A single instance of inconsistency can begin to build doubt about your trustworthiness.

When you think of some of the major brands you know, how do you think they have grown so huge? Many of these brands have built their empires through one simple idea. They offer a consistent product every time a customer purchases from their business. For instance, as you receive a call and you get to see the name of the person calling, there is usually something that describes the person that comes into your mind. We have renowned public figures in Africa that are well known for what they consistently fought for or achieved. Wangari Mathai was known as an environmentalist and Nelson Mandela as a freedom fighter in South Africa.

A Story of Resilience by Wheelchair Tennis Champion, Jane Ndenga

> I started playing tennis in 2012. My first participation in athletics was competing in Africa qualifiers which did not go well for me. I lost all my matches but I didn't get discouraged.

Jane was born normal, no complication, in Siaya County. She is the second-born in a family of five children. She was growing up well until she turned five years old when her life changed forever—polio paralysed her left leg; and not even the 12 surgical procedures that were perfomed on her rectified the condition. Her parents were determined to see her walk again, it never worked.

Jane had no option but to accept the life that fate had dealt her. She was physically and mentally tormented since she could no longer play with her peers. It took long before she could accept her situation. She was forced to undergo a series of counselling sessions. All the same, Jane kept her faith in God and moved on like others. She never thought of going to the streets to beg for money. She became a special needs child, in need of other people for support.

However, her parents did not enrol her in special needs schools for the physically challenged. She finished high school in 1995 and performed well. However, the journey had many challenges including being denied to participate in Physical Education exercises making her feel depressed.

> I was excluded in so many things. Sometimes I didn't feel needed because of my condition. Students and teachers thought I was there to take care of their stuff whenever they are doing rehearsals.

Despite the challenges, Jane did not give up. She raised her head high and remained focused on what she did. Her condition did not stop her from making choices of what she desired in life. After high school, she enrolled in a college where she studied public relations, front office, community counselling, and international business communication where she passed with a credit.

Jane began her sporting activities by playing wheelchair basketball before training on tennis. She had represented the Kenyan wheelchair basketball team in 2017 in South Africa. Apart from tennis and basketball, Jane also plays sitting volleyball as well as powerlifting. She served the volleyball team as the federation secretary-general from 2012 to 2016. In all her sporting activities, Jane has a passion in tennis that has made her travel internationally and met various people from other nations. She believes that her prayers to God enabled her to choose tennis as a career and has qualified for World Cup three times. The list of countries she went with her team for World Cup are the Netherlands in 2014 and 2018 as well as Italy in 2017. Apart from the two countries, Jane has managed to travel to South Africa, Bangkok, Ghana, and Nigeria through individual point tournaments called 'Futures' whereby International Tennis Federation sponsors their tours. The team also hosts the same events February every year in Kenya.

Challenges are part of life. Jane has also gone through ups and downs in her tennis career, one being funds.

> Challenges are many but the major one is on resources, I may wish to train more like every day but I can't. Sometimes it's so hard but I thank God who is always there to give me the grace to learn on how to save every amount I earn from tennis.

To her, getting a coach willing to train her without pay has made it difficult for her to train well. However, through self-motivation, the group has always trained without a coach especially when they do not have funds to facilitate their training.

> I always overcome by prayer and fasting. I get all my strength from my God who told me in his word that I can do all things through him who strengthens me. I want to sincerely thank our Government through the ministry of sports for always intervening in our situation.

Jane is always determined and consistent in her training. She has never given up her fight in overcoming challenges even when she is defeated. The game has instilled in her discipline and the need to concentrate on sharpening her skills as many players she began with, gave up on the way. She is grateful to her parents and siblings who have always supported her financially and spiritually. They have always believed in her even before winning a single match they had already named her a superstar.

The tennis champion applied for Wheelchair Tennis Council. She was lucky to be elected in August 2018 to represent Africa on issues pertaining to wheelchair tennis.

She also won sports Woman Living With Disability Award. Her team won the best team of the year in World Cup 2014. She has been able to achieve all this through the power of choice. She admits that God has been her reference whenever she wants to make a decision and has gone to the extent of fasting for three days.

> One of the hardest choices I made recently is when I was playing my futures in West Africa. I started my tournament in Nigeria but after the finals, I had some few days before the start of Ghana tournament. Thus I chose to have three days dry first. It was hard but I told God I must pray for me to perform well in the next finals.

CONCLUSION

Choose to be Great Today!

THE CHOICE TO change the level and perspective of life is yours. You don't have to be like everyone else; get out of this low level-thinking. People limit themselves to their current situation and cannot see beyond that. The time to eliminate limited perception is now. Greatness is a choice you can achieve so long as you keep in mind that you must wake up every day and demand for higher standard from your inner self. People who remain on the same level for a long time hold onto similar ideas and thoughts that make them lead mediocre lives. You have no choice but to separate yourself from such groups in order to live an independent prosperous life as we all have different destinies.

Always be among the top ten individuals who begin to strive for the highest possible level in all areas of their lives regarding spirituality, health, wealth, family, and abundance.

To advance from your present level, you have to start thinking and acting differently from the masses as well as having the determination and self-drive to succeed. People who lack focus settle for the crumbs that they are given. They are uncertain of what they want in life, so they just settle for anything on offer.

Lazy people make time for failure but they don't make time for success. They sit around expecting more from others, but they don't do anything to get things they want on their own.

You must start to think big all the time without limiting your dreams. The world says it's hard, but that's a lie, anything is possible. You can do whatever you want to do. You can be anything you want to be as long as you certainly believe in yourself.

Develop and grow yourself every day. Wake up and say: today I will be better than I was yesterday while you continually improve yourself. If you don't step up and live on a new level, you will be living on the low level of the majority. It takes no effort to be like everyone else as no effort is required to be average. Striving for greater heights takes courage, dedication, discipline and a continuous hunger to live a life according to your desire.

Breakaway from the masses that all think, act, and live in the same manner. Now is the time to challenge yourself to determine whether you are capable of achieving. You have everything within you to be successful keeping in mind that choice is what makes you great.

"

Character may determine our fate, but character is not determined by fate. It's determined by our choices. We must never forget how powerful character is in shaping our destiny. We must also remember how powerful we are in shaping our character.

"

Michael Josephson

WISE WORDS

The bad news is that time flies. The good news is you are the pilot.

Michael Ahshuler

One of the things I learned the hard way was that it doesn't pay to get discouraged. Keeping busy and making optimism a way of life can restore your faith in yourself.

Lucille Ball

A pessimist sees the difficulty in every opportunity; an optimist sees the opportunity in every difficulty.

Winston Churchill

Successful people do ordinary things with extraordinary consistency, commitment, and focus.

Jon Gordon

Change will not come if we wait for some other person, or if we wait for some other time. We are the ones we've been waiting for. We are the change that we seek.

Barack Obama

The best way to not feel hopeless is to get up and do something.

Barack Obama

If you're walking down the right path and you're willing to keep walking, eventually you'll make progress.

Barack Obama

To be born and to die is common to all but what makes the difference is what is between the two, life between when you were born and death. That's why choices matters.

John Abdub Wako

Leadership is a choice, not a position.

Stephen Covey

The self is not something ready-made, but something in continuous formation through choice of action

John Dewey

Its choice- not chance- that determines your destiny.

Jean Nidetch

What does CHOICE stand for?

C	–	Creating
H	–	Hope and
O	–	Opportunities
I	–	In
C	–	Character and
E	–	Education

ABOUT THE AUTHOR

Jᴏʜɴ Aʙᴅᴜʙ Wᴀᴋᴏ Bachelor's degree holder in Maritime Management from Moi University, Eldoret. He studied at Moi Forces Academy, Mombasa (2013) and Kenya Navy Primary (2009).

He was born in Marsabit County and is the second born in a family of six. He is a young and energetic motivational speaker, transformational leader, author, and a career advisor.

His other published work is *The Journey to Self-realization*.